Premarital And Singleness Curse Breaking

THIS BOOK IS INTENDED FOR ENGAGED COUPLES, SINGLES PLANNING TO GET MARRIED AND MARRIED COUPLES!

By Carlos A. Oliveira

HAVE ALL YOUR CURSES BROKEN AND DEMONS CAST OUT FIRST BEFORE MARRYING SOMEONE WHO ALSO HAS UNDERGONE THE SAME KIND OF INTENSIVE CURSE BREAKING DELIVERANCE PRAYERS.

Never ever marry anyone without both of you first undergo Premarital Curse Breaking. Why unite and combine your spouse's curses with yours, from both sides of your families, when you could enter into a marriage life curse free? Crimes, homicides, suicides, robbery, premature deaths, constant accidents, incurable diseases, alcoholism, corruption, drug dependency, poverty, sexual promiscuity and perversion, pedophilia, insanity, depression, domestic violence, adultery, divorce, etc., are all results of generations of curses residing in the family bloodline.

What can you do today to change this reality? What can you do today to make a difference in your children's lives to make sure they will have a safer and a better future than you had?

Start today, cast all curses and demons out of yourself and family and learn to keep them out, forever.

FIRST THINGS FIRST

Before beginning the process of breaking curses, always pray for protection first.

Here is a model of how you should pray:

"Father (Abba) in Heaven, in the name of the Lord Jesus Christ (Yahshua haMashiach) I ask that You forgive me of all sins I have committed against You and against your creation. I also ask You, Father, that you camp your angels around me and around all my family members, according to Your Word in Psalm 34:7, which says, "The angel of the Lord encamps around those who fear Him, and delivers them." (ESV), and also in Psalm 91:11-12, which says, "For He will command His angels concerning you to guard you in all your ways. On their hands they will bear you up, lest you strike your foot against a stone." (ESV). Thank You Father for protecting us and for camping your angels around us to keep us safe and protected against any form of attacks of the devils and his demons. We declare Isaiah 54:17, "No weapon formed against you (us) shall prosper." (NKJV). In Jesus Christ's Name I pray. Amen!

INTRODUCTION

Since curses are being precisely transferred from generation to generation, through the family bloodline and also from a person to another, from animals and objects to people and vise-versa, I have decided to put together this book in which I will unveil the darkness behind our families and societies and deal with these particular demons and curses, common to human beings, the proper way and help educate this generation already brainwashed and afflicted by such evil and sinful cultures, in most cases led by the television, movie and music industries as well as magazines, books, false religions, ungodly societies and organizations, new age spirituality, etc... that have been bombarding our children and young adults with all kinds of sinful, anti-Christ demonic messages and informations orchestrated, of course, by an invisible kingdom operating in the shadows that partially and conditionally rules over this planet which is known as Satan's kingdom.

SATAN AND HIS DEMONS WERE CAST DOWN TO THE EARTH

The Bible, in Revelation 12:7-12, gives us a pretty good idea on how this kingdom came about, it says,

"And war broke out in heaven: Michael and his angels fought with the dragon; and the dragon and his angels fought, but they did not prevail, nor was a place found for them in heaven any longer. So the great dragon was cast out, that serpent of old, called the Devil and Satan, who deceives the whole world; he was cast to the earth, and his angels were cast out with him. Then I heard a loud voice saying in heaven, 'Now salvation, and strength, and the kingdom of our God, and the power of His Christ have come, for the accuser of our brethren, who accused them before our God day and night, has been cast down. And they overcame him by the blood of the Lamb and by the word of their testimony, and they did not love their lives to the death. Therefore rejoice, O heavens, and you who dwell in them! Woe to the inhabitants of the earth and the sea! For the devil has come down to you, having great wrath, because he knows that he has a short time.'" Revelation 12:7-12 (NKJV).

The good news is that the Word of God gives us strategies on how to overcome Satan's army, right here on earth, and be able to live in victory and without fear of evil.

PEOPLE ARE ALREADY BORN WITH CURSES

Generational curses are the ones passed down from generation to generation, through the family bloodline. The Bible does mention "generational curses" in several places including Exodus 20:5, "I the LORD thy God am a jealous God, visiting the iniquity of the fathers upon the children unto the third and fourth generation."; Exodus 34:7, " keeping mercy for thousands, forgiving iniquity and transgression and sin, by no means clearing the guilty, visiting the iniquity of the fathers upon the children and the children's children to the third and the fourth generation."; Numbers 14:18, " The Lord is longsuffering and abundant in mercy, forgiving iniquity and transgression; but He by no means clears the guilty, visiting the iniquity of the fathers on the children to the third and fourth generation."; Deuteronomy 5:8-9, "You shall not make for yourself a carved image—any likeness of anything that is in heaven above, or that is in the earth beneath, or that is in the water under the earth; 9 you shall not bow down to them nor serve them. For I, the Lord your God, am a jealous God, visiting the iniquity of the fathers upon the children to the third and fourth generations of those who hate Me"; etc. God warns us that He is a jealous God, punishing the children for the sin of the fathers to the third and fourth generation of those who hate Him. Now taking that analogy into consideration we understand that human beings are already being born with curses they inherit from their ancestors.

CAN CHRISTIANS HAVE DEMONS?

People frequently ask me these questions, "Can Christians have demons on the inside? Can the Holy Spirit and demons share the same space in a Christian's body?"

Well, let me answer it by asking a couple of questions, "Can the Holy Spirit watch pornography with Christians? Can the Holy Spirit watch sexual and violent movies on TV with Christians? Can the Holy Spirit partake in gossiping and judging others with Christians? Can the Holy Spirit fornicate with Christians while dating?" Well, if you consider yourself a Christian and practice such things, then you'll need to repent, ask God to forgive you then cast those your devils out of your body first to make room for the Holy Spirit to come in and dwell in it. Don't you agree?

ADULTERY, MASTURBATION, LUST AND FORNICATION

Dating spiced up with erotic kisses, hugs and body touches is crossing the line, it will cause harm, pain and distress in the long run since ground for torment has been granted to the devil. Even dating without sex is a form of "adultery". Matt 5:28, "But I say unto you, that whosoever looks on a woman to lust after her has committed adultery with her already in his heart." What kind of thoughts do you think comes after kisses and hugs in a premarital intimate relationship? By the way, intimate dating is not Biblical, it's Hollywoodical.

Matthew 5:27-28 "You have heard that it was said, 'You shall not commit adultery'; but I say to you that everyone who looks at a woman with lust for her has already committed adultery with her in his heart." (NKJV)

Let me ask you a question now, if you masturbate do you visualize or think of a tree or a piece of concrete or you think of or visualize a naked person or people or animals instead?
If you are still a little bit confused regarding this then read the above scriptures again and let the Holy Spirit speak to you! Remember if the world approves it, including hollywood, then run away from it, as fast as you can.

CAN THE MARRIAGE BED BE DEFILED?

The use of contraceptives as well as oral and anal sex, the use of sex toys, watch pornography secretly or even together as a couple will open doors for demons to gain entrance into the marital life causing serious troubles that may result in adultery, separation and divorce. Homicide, suicide, severe health issues and financial ruin may be the end result of it.

DEMONIC SEXUAL LUST

We human beings were created by God with natural sexual desires for multiplication purpose; Gen 1:28, "Be fruitful and multiply". Natural sexual desire meaning we can exercise self-control over temptations. On the other hand uncontrollable sexual lust drives people to do evil things, stupid things and most the time making people feel powerless and unable to subdue such a strong sexual appetite, to make things much worse television, internet, magazines, etc., have been fueling the problem with sexual related shows, movies, photos of naked and semi-naked people and so on and so forth. This form of uncontrollable sexual lust is demonic in nature, it's a combination of demons and curses working together with the purpose of destroying those driven by it.

If you are being driven by tormenting sexual thoughts and desires and are not able to exercise self-control to resist them, then, yes, you are being oppressed and somewhat manipulated by these forces of darkness that perhaps have found openings in your life which they claim as "ground for torment" or "legal ground". Anything that drives a person to do evil and breaks God's laws has the finger of the devil in it.

DEMONS HAVE TO BE CAST OUT, NOT PRAYED AWAY!

Folks, one of the greatest misunderstanding, in the body of Christ, is concerning deliverance. Many pastors and teachers have been teaching their congregations that prayer and attending church services regularly are all they need to defeat the enemy of their souls, no wonder most of these leaders are also getting hit themselves by evil forces dwelling here on earth.

In Mark 16:17, Jesus went on to say that certain signs were to follow the believers, which includes the casting out of demons. Jesus Himself, many times, drove out demons too to prove to us that evil spirits are real and very present in this world. He also gave us authority to trample these devils and to overcome all the power of the enemy (Luke 10:19).

TRANSFERENCE OF SPIRITS

Common ways of demonic transferences happen through datings, sexual promiscuity, immorality, bestiality, ungodly friendships, relationships between people, also between people and animals as well as between people and inanimate objects and also through communication and interaction with spirits and even dead people.

Not too long ago a woman who appeared on a reality television series, in which I was a part of, said that her greatest addiction in life was her own breasts. They were very large breasts, each one larger than her own head. Another person, on the same documentary, confessed that he was in love with his automobile.

All of these strange occurrencies are already forms of demonic possession. In the case of the woman with very large breasts there were already demons lodged in her breasts making her fall in love with and lust after them. These are manifestations of what is known as "sexual demons" and they even have the ability to supernaturally enlarge sexual body parts to make people lust after and feel in love with them.

When people develop close relationships with others who are under severe demonic oppression then they run the risk of having some of those demons transferred to them. It happen more often than we realize and no one is immune to this kind of attacks.

TRANSFERENCE OF SPIRITS FROM DECEASED HUMAN BEINGS

I was called to assist a young lady once who became possessed at a friend's funeral. She reported that while she was near the casket she then felt something heavy entering her body and she knew exactly where the heaviness came from. She then began having some of the same simptoms and manifestations that her deceased friend used to have and from that moment on she was not the same anymore.

Another woman had asked me to visit her, in Beverly Hills, back in September 2013, she reported that she heard voices, non-stop, tormenting her day and night, 24 hours a day, 7 days a week. During my investigation of the problem she then said that everything started when she visited a deceased celebrity's grave, at a nearby cemetery, and then inquired of the dead female singer as to how she had died, since it was a mystery even to this day. This lady then reported to me that she visited the grave three times total and on the third time then the voices began tormenting her saying that they were the singer's friends and so forth.

On another occasion, a young mother of three children reported to me that after her father had passed away, while in prison, then they began having paranormal activities in her home with ghost apparitions and objects moving around in the house and so forth. Then I asked her if she had brought home any of the father's belongings, etc., then she reported that she didn't have any of his belongings at home, only his ashes because she had not spent much time with him, then she thought it would be a nice thing to do to have his remains staying at the house, to show love and appreciation for her father. At that very moment I told her that the father's remains had brought the demons that killed him in prison into her home, to prey upon the next victim in the family.

People have no idea how the demonic realm operates as they go in life opening up doors for these creatures to come in, torment and destroy them.

DATING AND FRIENDSHIPS

Some of the most common ways of demonic transference happen through close relationships between people, especially through datings, premarital sexual relationships, etc. Everybody has issues, curses and demons and when someone comes in a close intimate relationship with another demon-oppressed human being then demons will simply unite their forces and begin working against both parties to torment and destroy them and make their lives miserable for years to come.

Demons are smart creatures, they have been around way longer than we have, plus, for the most part, they are invisible to the naked eye and that makes things much easier for them to attack us without being detected. They know everything about human weaknesses and know exactly where to push the "buttons" to make our lives go down hill very fast.

In order for us to put a stop to these demonic entities and activities we must follow God's guindace found only in His Word, which is the Bible. The infallible Word of God has answers for everything under the sun.

DATING AND THE BASTARD CURSE

Deuteronomy 23:2 "One of illegitimate birth shall not enter the assembly of the Lord; even to the tenth generation none of his descendants shall enter the assembly of the Lord." Adulterous dating has been playing a major role in keeping the curse of the bastard well alive today and for generations to come, being one of the causes of major social disasters, mass murders, killings, destruction, family division, high and low level corruptions, abortion which is a form of human sacrifice, etc

CULTURAL CURSES: TATTOOS AND BODY PIERCINGS:

Leviticus 19:28 (NKJV)

"You shall not make any cuttings in your flesh for the dead, nor tattoo any marks on you: I am the Lord."

Some of the ways demons enter people's bodies or transfer from one to another are through tattoos, body cuttings and piercings. Demons know that everytime one of God's principals and statutes are broken the they can gain access to one's life, leading a person into, what it seems like, a never-ending road of destruction, pain, agony and torment among other things.

-BIBLE DRESS CODE:

Deuteronomy 22:5 (NKJV)

"A woman shall not wear anything that pertains to a man, nor shall a man put on a woman's garment, for all who do so are an abomination to the Lord your God.

Here is a great example of how movies, television, Hollywood and music have been playing a key role in influencing our culture. They always seem to promote as "cool" and "fun" everything that God condemns in His Word. The more Godless the culture is the better. These ones too are infesting people and families with demons and curses.

GHOST HUNTING SHOWS; SEXUAL, HORROR AND VIOLENT MOVIES, DEMONIC MUSIC, ETC.

Another way people are getting hit by curses and demons are through certain types of television shows, soap operas, movies, etc. Paranormal ghost hunting shows are door openers to demonic activies in a house and family. Besides they also teach people wrong ways of dealing with the unseen world, they portray that it's okey to communicate with dark spirits, to cleanse a house with sage, to record electronic voice phenomena (evp) and so foth. No, it not okey to dialogue with spirits, it's not okey to smudge sage in a house, it's not okey to record evps . These practices will grant demons more ground for torment.

YOUR FAMILY IS UNDER CURSE, NOW WHAT?

To come out from under generational curses one must be a born again believer in Jesus Christ. Through Him only and through and His sacrifice for us, humans, can curses be broken.

Galatians 3:13 says, "Christ has redeemed us from the curse of the law, having become a curse for us (born-again Christians) for it is written, 'Cursed is everyone who hangs on a tree'"

Romans 10:7, "If you confess with your mouth 'Jesus is Lord' and believe in your heart that God raised Him from the dead, you'll be saved.

Jesus Christ said in John 14:6, "I am the Way, the Truth and the Life, no one comes to the Father but by Me". Through Jesus Christ only we can be saved and forgiven and through Him only we can overcome curses and demons. Amen?

The good news is Jesus Christ gave us His authority to defeat the kingdom of Satan on earth, Luke 10:19, "I have given you authority to trample on snakes and scorpions and to overcome all the power of the enemy, nothing will harm you". In order for all curses to be broken in our lives we must make sure Jesus Christ is our only Lord and Savior, shut all the demonic doors that we previously had opened to demons, then renounce and break curses and cast out all demons associated with them. Remember we can be saved and still go on in life cursed and demonized.

BREAKING SOUL-TIE CURSES:

Now it is very important that you verbally renounce, cancel and break all soul-ties you developed with anyone that you had intimate relatioship with, including ex-dates, ex-spouses, ex-lovers, and even with close friends who were addicted to drugs, alcohol, nicotine, pornography, etc. If you don't remember everyone's names then break the ties by saying "with all people I had relationships with, etc".
Start out by saying, In the name of Jesus Christ, according to Luke 10:19, which says, "I have given you authority to trample on snakes and scorpions and to overcome all the power of the enemy, nothing will harm you." I now renounce, cancel and break all evil, demonic and ungodly soul-ties I

developed with _____, _____, _____, (fill the blanks with everyone's names that you can remember of) and all other sexual partners, friends, animals, objects, sex toys, idols such as, tv celebrities, singers, actors, athletes, tv shows, paranormal ghost hunting shows, horror movies, cars, dolls, toys, occultic objects, spirit guides, angels, demons, etc... In the name of Jesus Christ I now clear myself of all impurity I inherited from those relatioships and I command all of you, demons, to leave me and my family now, in the name of Jesus Christ.

RENOUNCING COMMON DEMONIC LEGAL GROUNDS AND OPEN DOORS:

Deuteronomy 18:9-12 (NKJV)

"When you come into the land which the Lord your God is giving you, you shall not learn to follow the abominations of those nations. There shall not be found among you anyone who makes his son or his daughter pass through the fire, or one who practices witchcraft, or a soothsayer, or one who interprets omens, or a sorcerer, or one who conjures spells, or a medium, or a spiritist, or one who calls up the dead. For all who do these things are an abomination to the Lord, and because of these abominations the Lord your God drives them out from before you."

Folks, now take the time to renounce one by one of the demonic legal grounds below. You may not have done all of them, but on behalf of your family bloodline you should do it anyway. Just say it out loud, Father in Heaven, in the name of my Lord Jesus Christ I ask you that you forgive me of all the sins I have committed against you and against those you created. Father, do not remember the iniquities of my forefathers against me and my family (Psalm 79:8), in the mighty name of Jesus Christ, I pray amen.

Father in the name of the Lord Jesus Christ, according to Luke 10:19, Matthew 10:1 and Mark 16:17, on behalf of myself and my family I now renounce, cancel and break all assignments of the devil against us that came to us through demonic gates and doors we've opened. In the name of Jesus Christ I now renounce, cancel and break:

Astral Projection, Séances, Light as a Feather, Table Lifting, Ouija Board, Bloody Mary, Spells, Telepathy, Handwriting Analysis, Automatic

Handwriting, Spirit Guides, Fortune Telling, Tarot Cards, Palm Reading, Witchcraft, Sorcery, Divination, Levitation, Trances, Satanism, Magic Eight Ball, Ouija Board, Pendulum, Hypnotism, Consulting With Psychics and Mediums, Astrology/Horoscopes, Black & White Magic, Dungeons & Dragons, Blood pacts, Cutting Oneself on Purpose, Objects of Worship, Talisman, Necromancy, Water Witching, Incantation, Charms, Fetishes, Voodoo, Cleansing Rituals and Ceremonies, Healing Crystals, Healing Stones, Sage Smudging, Candle Burning, Incense Burning, EVPs, Sex with Spirits, Dialoguing and Communicating with Spirits, Consulting with the Dead or Familiar Spirits, Mysticism, Sensei Devotion Through Martial Arts, Superstitions, New Age Spirituality, Freemasonry, Mind Science Cults, Silva Mind Control, Hare Krishna, Roy Master, Unitarianism, Universalism, Humanism, Hinduism, Buddhism, Zen Buddhism, Bahaism, Ritualism, Formalism, Legalism, Atheism, Spiritism, Taoism, Confucianism, Shintoism, Native American Worship, Islam, Black Muslim, Rosicrucianism, Occult Video Games, Violent Video Games, Watching Ghost Hunting Shows and Movies, TV Shows, Violent Movies, Sexual Movies, Horror Movies, Pornography, Tattoo, Sexual Promiscuity, Contraceptives, Abortion, etc.

CAST OUT COMMON DEMON GROUPINGS:

Folks, now take the time to cast out one by one of the demons and strongholds below. You may not have all of them in you, but on behalf of yourself and your family bloodline you should do it anyway. Just say it out loud, in the name of my Lord Jesus Christ I now exercise authority over the kingdom of darkness attacking myself and my family, according to Luke 10:19, which says, "I have given you authority to trample on snakes and scorpions and to overcome all the power of the enemy, nothing will harm you". Also according to Matthew 10:1, which says, "Jesus Christ gave His disciples (His Church) power to drive out demons and to heal all kinds of sickness and all kinds of deseases". Also according to Mark 16:17, "This signs will follow those who believe, in my name they will drive out demons". I now command you demons of _____, _____, _____, (fill the blanks with the list below) , come out now, In Jesus' mighty name and never come back. Get out of me now and get out of my all family members, get out of my family bloodline, in the name of Jesus Christ my Lord and Savior.

Bitterness, Nervousness, Resentment, Hatred, Unforgiveness, Rage, Irritability, Intolerance, Violence, Temper, Anger, Retaliation, Murder, Worries, Anxiety, Dread, Apprehension, Escape, Insecurity, Inferiority, Depression, Panic Attacks, Agoraphobia, Fear of Disapproval, Failure Mindset, Rejection Mindset, Insanity, Extreme Sensitiveness, Despair, Self-Delusion, Despondency, Discouragement, Defeatism, Dejection, Hopelessness, Suicide, Insomnia, Rebellion, Strife, Control, Manipulation, Possessiveness, Dominance, Retaliation, Contention, Bickering, Argument, Quarreling, Fighting, Destruction, Stubbornness, Disobedience, Accusation, Fear of Rejection, Negative Emotions, Rejection, Self-Rejection, Extreme Jealousy, Envy, Lying, Deceit, Withdrawal, Extreme Passivity, Heaviness, Gloom, Burden, Persecution, Mental Illness, Schizophrenia, Paranoia, Confusion, Indecision, Self-Deception, Self-Hatred, Mind-Binding, Idolatry, Phobias, Hysteria, Tiredness, Weariness, Laziness, Fear of Man, Fear of Satan, Pride, Ego, Vanity, Self-Righteousness, Haughtiness, Importance, Arrogance, Affectation, Covetousness, Stealing, Kleptomania, Materialism, Greed, Sophistication, Perfectionism, Competitions, Impatience, False Compassion, Extended Grief and Sorrow, Cruelty, Fatigue, Anorexia, Bulimia, Infirmity, Sickness, Disease, Premature Death, Emotional Disorder, Hyper-Activity, Restlessness, Cursing, Blasphemy, Gossip, Criticism, Backbiting, Mockery, Belittling, Nicotine, Alcohol Addiction, Drug Use and Abuse, Medication Dependency and Abuse, Caffeine Addiction, Gluttony, Sexual Impurity, Sexual Perversion, Unnatural Sexual Practices, Child Molestation, Uncontrollable Sexual Desires, Compulsive Masturbation, Fantasy Lust, Sodomy, Adultery, Fornication, Incest, Harlotry, Rape, Exposure, Frigidity, Bestiality, Religious Doctrinal Error, Fear of Lost Salvation, Fear of Hell, Seduction, Murder, Abortion.

BREAKING GENERATIONAL CURSES:

In the name of Jesus Christ, according to Luke 10:19, Matthew 10:1 and Mark 16:17, as it relates to me and my family, I now exercise authority over all demonic spirits, principalities, powers and curses that have been plaguing my family bloodline for generations. I commend you now evil spirits behind all inherited sins, bastard curse, genetic disorders, cellular disorders, character defects, personality traits, learned demonic inner vows, evil ties. I break all curses and put the Blood of Jesus Christ in their places. I cancel all generational curses back to the beginning of time and all present and future generations. By the power of the Name of Jesus Christ, I now confess that my family and I are curse free, for the glory of the Almighty God.

In the name of my Lord and Savior Jesus Christ, as it relates to me and my family, I cast out all evil spirits of anger, hatred, rage, pride, defiance, persecution, prejudice, judgment, gossip, rebellion, disobedience, arrogance, hypocrisy, unforgiveness, envy, impatience, resentment, vanity, coveting, selfishness, idolatry, haughtiness, mockery, murder, infirmity, sickness, disease, insanity, depression, oppression, suicide, schizophrenia, hormonal disorders, denial, disbelief, betrayal, guilt, confusion, shame, revenge, doubt, self-hatred, poor self-image, rejection, anorexia, bulimia, possessiveness; deaf, dumb, blind and mute spirits; fear of man, fear of Satan, fear of ghosts, fear of dead people, agoraphobia, timidity, passivity, control, unbelief, jealousy, division, disunity, distrust, deception, dishonesty, destruction, vengeance, hyperactivity, competitiveness, accusation, torment, procrastination, stubbornness, strife, criticism, manipulation, materialism, greed, poverty, divorce, separation, hypochondria, or dysfunction, fatigue, worry, anxiety, sleeplessness, ADD, ADHD, escape, withdrawal, loneliness, isolation, nervousness, negativety, all addictions, gluttony, nicotine, alcoholism, perfection, excessive spending, consumerism, gambling, drug abuse, self-cutting, self-multilation, body piercing, tattoos, self-abuse, yoga, transcedental meditation, sexual perversion, masturbation, seduction, fornication, adultery, pornography, lust, incest, pedophilia, sodomy, unnatural sexuality, homophobia, sexual impotency, sexual immorality and impurity, bestiality, abortion, sexual promiscuity, demonic games, sleeping spirits, new age demons, cult and occult spirits and seducing evil spirits. I command you all demons, devils and curses to leave me and my family members now, in the mighty name of Jesus Christ.

In the Name of Jesus Christ, I renounce, break and destroy all kinds of spells, curses, voodoo, witchcraft, black and white magics, vexes, hexes, occult; masonic rituals, sacrifices and blood convenants; satanic sacrifices, rituals and blood covenants; demonic activities of all kinds and forms; coven practices, sacrifices and rituals; evil wishes, all forms of occult involvement, Islamic fasting prayers, word cursing and evil judgments that have been passed down through my family bloodline. I cast you all out now devils, demons and curses, get out now, in the mighty name of Jesus Christ. Father in Heaven, I ask you forgiveness for as I renounce all evil inner oaths, vows and judgements made by myself and by my ancestors. I ask you Father, in the name of my Lord Jesus Christ that you break, cancel and destroy all evil oaths, vows and judgements and from any curse they may have held us in. Lord, in the name of Jesus Christ, forgive us of the iniquities and sins of ancestors against me and my family.

In the name of our Lord Jesus Christ I break, cancel and destroy all curses resulting in the destruction of the body and mind, behavioral disorder and perversion; lies, blasphemies, enchantments, encantations, sorceries, communication with dark spirits, consulting with the dead, condemnation, control, curses from the womb, strongholds affecting the family, curses from any demonic doors that we have opened to demons, curses from my family bloodline from both my father's and the my mother's ancestral family bloodlines, word cursing others; illusions and delusions; demonic activities, influences and attacks; demonic condemnation, demonic covenants, depression, insanity, mental illness, anger, rage, hatred, destruction of finances, marriage separation, destruction of family, destruction of the body, distractions, dullness of mind, dysfunctionality, adverse effects, every word cursing spoken contrary to God's plans and purposes for my life and family, demonic condemnation, evil contracts, evil plans, evil powers, hindrances, evil influences passed down, emotionally, spiritually, socially, inherited, or any other channel, unknown to me, evil alliances, and evil thoughts and spoken words concerning me and my family, demons that follow and harass; demonic strongholds, trauma, familiar perversion, financial curses, futility of the mind, ill spoken words, interaction and communication with evil spirits, manipulation, demonic mindset demonic mind control, neutralizing effects, bad habits, poverty, evil soul-ties, oppressive feelings, oppression, perverse speech, pains; oppressive, evil and negative thoughts; spiritual wickedness, religious error, satanic, and demonic alliances, schemes of the enemy or wicked people, self condemnation, sexual perversion, spiritual corruption, evil systems of people, twistedness of the mind, ungodly associations or covenants with evil people, terrorism, unrighteous pacts and agreements, witchcraft spells, evil thinking patterns.

Father in Heaven, in the name of the Lord Jesus Christ I ask you now that you put an end to all generations and relational curses that have plagued my family bloodline. Thak you Father for forgiving us and for removing all unrighteousness from our DNAs. Thank you Father for releasing your blessings now to follow me and my family, my descendants for as long as we remain on this planet. Thank you father for cleansing us of all impurity, perversion and corruption, in the mighty name of Jesus Christ. Father, grant us to live under your total guidance, protection, property, health and spiritual blessings, in the mighty name of Jesus Christ I pray. I now declare that, through God's grace, my family is now curse free. Amen.

Folks, I recommend that this ministration be performed individually by all those committed to start their families, as married couples, curse free, at least seven times within the next six months, with all honesty, whether they are engaged couples, singles planning to get married or married couples.

LEVITICUS 18 - LAWS OF SEXUAL MORALITY

Then the Lord spoke to Moses, saying, "Speak to the children of Israel, and say to them: 'I am the Lord your God. According to the doings of the land of Egypt, where you dwelt, you shall not do; and according to the doings of the land of Canaan, where I am bringing you, you shall not do; nor shall you walk in their ordinances. You shall observe My judgments and keep My ordinances, to walk in them: I am the Lord your God. You shall therefore keep My statutes and My judgments, which if a man does, he shall live by them: I am the Lord.

'None of you shall approach anyone who is near of kin to him, to uncover his nakedness: I am the Lord. The nakedness of your father or the nakedness of your mother you shall not uncover. She is your mother; you shall not uncover her nakedness. The nakedness of your father's wife you shall not uncover; it is your father's nakedness. The nakedness of your sister, the daughter of your father, or the daughter of your mother, whether born at home or elsewhere, their nakedness you shall not uncover. The nakedness of your son's daughter or your daughter's daughter, their nakedness you shall not uncover; for theirs is your own nakedness. The nakedness of your father's wife's daughter, begotten by your father—she is your sister—you shall not uncover her nakedness. You shall not uncover the nakedness of your father's sister; she is near of kin to your father. You shall not uncover the nakedness of your mother's sister, for she is near of kin to your mother. You shall not uncover the nakedness of your father's brother. You shall not approach his wife; she is your aunt. You shall not uncover the nakedness of your daughter-in-law—she is your son's wife—you shall not uncover her nakedness. You shall not uncover the nakedness of your brother's wife; it is your brother's nakedness. You shall not uncover the nakedness of a woman and her daughter, nor shall you take her son's daughter or her daughter's daughter, to uncover her nakedness. They are near of kin to her. It is wickedness. Nor shall you take a woman as a rival to her sister, to uncover her nakedness while the other is alive. 'Also you shall not approach a woman to uncover her nakedness as long as she is in her customary impurity. Moreover you shall not lie carnally with your neighbor's wife, to defile yourself with her. And you shall not let any of your descendants pass through the fire to Molech, nor shall you profane the name of your God: I am the Lord. You shall not lie with a male as with a woman. It is an abomination. Nor shall you mate with any animal, to defile yourself with it. Nor shall any woman stand before an animal to mate with it. It is perversion.

'Do not defile yourselves with any of these things; for by all these the nations are defiled, which I am casting out before you. For the land is defiled; therefore I visit the punishment of its iniquity upon it, and the land vomits out its inhabitants. You shall therefore keep My statutes and My judgments, and shall not commit any of these abominations, either any of your own nation or any stranger who dwells among you (for all these abominations the men of the land have done, who were before you, and thus the land is defiled), lest the land vomit you out also when you defile it, as it vomited out the nations that were before you. For whoever commits any of these abominations, the persons who commit them shall be cut off from among their people.

'Therefore you shall keep My ordinance, so that you do not commit any of these abominable customs which were committed before you, and that you do not defile yourselves by them: I am the Lord your God.'"

*Scriptures taken by permission from New King James Version (NKJV)

SINGLENESS CURSE BREAKING PRAYER

INTENSIVE CURSE BREAKING PRAYER

Right now you are about to verbally minister the breaking of curses of singleness and others over yourself, which also include: separation, divorce, adultery, loneliness, depression, domestic violence, sexual perversion, witchcraft, etc.

If you happen to be under this curse, the curse of singleness, or if perhaps this curse runs in your family bloodline, you may feel some manifestations as evil spirits and curses behind singleness are being addressed.

You may feel some demonic manifestations happening in your body, it can occur in the form of dizziness, you may feel nauseous. It can be constant coughing, belching; it can be things moving inside your body, it can be pain, such as muscle spasm, headache, back pain, stomach ache, abdominal pain, etc.

You were just fine then all of a sudden, during this ministration, you got this pain and/or heaviness and/or pressure out of nowhere. In some cases the pain may feel like a stabbing sensation, as if you were literally being stabbed by someone, that is pretty much what can happen.

There are some other cases where nothing seems to occur, but that doesn't mean there are no spirits or curses in you, demons can hide for while when given opportunities to do so.

If you happen to be under the curse of singleness, then I have some other recommendations at the end of this book. Now make sure to read the following prayer out loud, if you can.

FIRST THINGS FIRST

The Bible says in the Book of Luke, chapter 10, verse 19, "I have given you authority to trample on snakes and scorpions and to overcome all the power of the enemy and nothing will harm you". The Bible also says in the Book of Matthew, chapter 10, verse 1 that Jesus Christ called to himself his twelve disciples, which are the Believers today, and he gave them power to drive out demons and to heal all kinds of sickness and all kinds of diseases. The Bible also says in the Book of Mark, chapter 16, verse 17, "These signs will follow those who believe in my name they will drive out evil spirits". The Bible also says in the Book of Matthew, chapter 16, verse 19, "Whatever you bind on Earth in bound in Heaven, whatever you loose on Earth is loosed in Heaven". The Bible also says in James, chapter 4, verse 7, "Submit yourself to the Lord, resist the Devil and he will flee from you".

In the name of the Lord Jesus Christ, I now exercise authority over every demonic spirit, principalities and powers assigned against me to come out right now.

In the name of the Lord Jesus Christ I now command the generational curse of singleness, evil spirits working to keep me alone and lonely, in the name of the Lord Jesus Christ, I command you now to come up to the surface now. Come up to the surface, evil spirits, come up here, in Jesus' mighty name.

I command now the demons behind the curse of singleness, I command you now to surface in the name of Jesus Christ. Surface now in the name of Jesus Christ. Come up to the surface evil spirits, in the mighty name of the Lord Jesus Christ.

Now devils, I am going to restrain you and drive you out, and as I restrain you and drive you out, you are going to leave my body and leave me alone, that is what the deal is. I am going to cast you out now evil spirits, you'll have to go.

In the name of the Lord Jesus Christ, I now exercise authority over you spirits behind singleness curse. I now bind and restrain you according to Matthew 16:19, I command you now to come out me, come out singleness curse, come out evil spirits. I command you now to come out, come out in Jesus' mighty name. Come out loneliness demons, come out demons assigned to keep me single and alone for life, in the name of Jesus Christ, I command you now to get out, I command you now to get out of me.

Broken marriage demons, I command you now to get out of my family bloodline, come out broken marriage demons and curses, in the name of Jesus Christ. You divorce devils get out now, divorce demons get out of me now, divorce curse come out, come out divorce and separation, come out divorce curse in the name of the Lord Jesus Christ. I command you devils get out now. Demons behind divorce, separation, legal separation, I now command you to come out evil spirits, come out of me and out my family bloodline now, get out of me now, in the name of the Jesus Christ. Come out, come out, come out demons, come out demons, get out now, get out now, come out, come out, come out, come out, come out, come out, come out, in the name of Jesus Christ, I command you now come out, in the name of Jesus Christ.

Spirits behind sexual perversion, adultery curses and demons, I command you now to come out of me, get out of me now and out of my family bloodline. Get out of my DNA. I command you now to come out adultery, in Jesus' name. Adultery demons come out, sexual demons come out now, come out sexual perversion, come out in Jesus' mighty name. Pornography come out in the name of Jesus Christ. Adultery devils, I command you now to get out of me, get out adultery. Adultery curse and demons go straight to the pit now, get out of me and go straight to the abyss now, in Jesus' name.

Demons behind loneliness, loneliness demons, isolation devils, I command you now to get out of me right now, come out, come out, come out, in the name of Jesus Christ, I command you now to come out. In the name of Jesus Christ I command you now to come out. In the name of Jesus Christ I command you now to come out, get out now. Isolation, come out now, loneliness devils I command you now to go straight to the abyss, in Jesus' name.

Come out singleness curse, come out singleness curse, get out now, up and out, up and out, up and out, up and out, in Jesus' name. Curse of singleness, up and out, in the name of Jesus Christ. Divorce curse come out, legal separation demons come out, separation demons come out, domestic violence demons come out in the name of Jesus Christ. Domestic abuse, and violence come out, verbal abuse, in the name of Jesus Christ. Violence I command you now to come out of my and my family bloodline, in the name of Jesus Christ. Verbal abuse and violence against women and children I command you now to come out, come out now demons, come out now devils, come out now curses, in Jesus' name.

Family separation, separation curse I command you now to come out. Divorce demons, get out, broken marriage demons come out, broken marriage devils come out, in the name of the Lord Jesus Christ. Marriage unhappiness, I command you now to come out, get out now unhappiness, unsatisfaction, I command you now to get out, unhappiness get out, depression come out of me and out of my family bloodline, in the name of Jesus Christ.

Marital loneliness and depression I command you now to come out. Marital depression get out now in the name of Jesus Christ, come out now in the name of Jesus Christ. I command you now to go straight to the abyss. I command you now to go straight to the abyss. I command you now to go straight to the abyss in the mighty name of Jesus Christ, get out now, come out now, in the name of Jesus Christ.

I have authority on Earth to break curses and to cast out demons, given to me by Jesus Christ, my Lord and Savior, which is recorded in the Book of Luke, chapter 10, verse 19, and Mark 16:17. I have authority to overcome all the power of the Devil given to me by Jesus Christ. Now demons, I command you now to get out, come out now singleness curse, come out now generational curses of singleness in the name of Jesus Christ. Infertility curses and demons, get out of me now, come out, come out, come out, come out, curses I break you now in Jesus' name, you are now broken and destroyed forever. Curses of singleness you are now broken in the name of the Lord Jesus Christ. I uproot every demon and every devil now trying to keep me alone, lonely and isolated, in the name of the Jesus Christ, get out demons, get out demons, get out demons, get out demons, come out now, come out now, come out now, come out in the name of Jesus Christ.

Curse of divorce, I command you now to come out. Divorce and separation, get out now devils, I command you now to come out in the name of the Jesus Christ. In the name of the Lord Jesus Christ, I now break the curse of living together without being legally married, I command you now to come out demons. Come out now, living together devils come out now, living together demons and curses get out now, in the mighty name of the Lord Jesus Christ.

Curses of witchcraft and voodoo, come out of me and my family bloodline, come out, come out, come out, come out in the name of the Lord Jesus Christ, evil spirits. I command you now to go straight to the abyss. I command you now to go straight to the abyss. I command you now to go straight to the abyss in the mighty name of Jesus Christ.

Singleness curse and all the demons attached to you, get out now and go straight to the abyss, go straight to the abyss, go straight to the abyss, in the mighty name of the Lord Jesus Christ my Lord and Savior.

I now uproot all witchcraft, voodoo, black magic, witchcraft spells cast on me and on my family to separate us and to keep us single, separated and divorced, in the name of Jesus Christ I command all these witchcraft now to get out. Witchcraft demons and curses, come out, witchcraft come out, witchcraft come out. I uproot you witchcraft, I have authority to break all kinds of witchcraft, therefore I break you now in the name of Jesus Christ. I break you now witchcraft, voodoo, black magic, hexes, vexes and word cursing, in Jesus' mighty name, you are now broken, in Jesus' name.

Every witchcraft done against me and my family is now broken and destroyed, in the mighty name of the Lord Jesus Christ, in the mighty name of the Lord Jesus Christ, I declare you broken and destroyed, in the mighty name of the Lord Jesus Christ my Lord and Savior.

Evil spirits go straight to the abyss now, all of you. Come out curses of singleness, come out in the name of Jesus Christ. I command you now to go straight to the abyss in the mighty name of Jesus Christ my Lord and Savior. Amen!

CLOSING PRAYER

Father in Heaven, I ask you right now to seal this deliverance and that you fill every empty spot vacated by unclean spirits with the presence of the Holy Spirit in this my body, mind, soul and spirit, in the name of Jesus Christ, my Lord and Savior. Amen!

Let's put an end to all these curses that have been destroying people, plaguing entire families and generations of innocent human beings everywhere.

May the LORD bless you and your family!

Brother Carlos A. Oliveira

Visit us on the web at www.brothercarlos.org

***All Scripture quotations, unless otherwise indicated, were taken from the New King James Version of The Bible by Thomas Nelson Publishers. Used by permission.

Made in the USA
San Bernardino, CA
04 June 2017